The following writings are drawn from my own experiences. Please be warned that some subjects may trigger negative emotions in individuals. Remember, to step away, make some tea, go outside, and breathe. This collection is about breaking down and stepping into one's own power. I hope you enjoy it as much as I enjoyed writing it.

Anjelica

I am Lost

With you,

there was always

something missing.

A rock left unturned.

A tune unsung.

Your hands

held too

tightly.

If only they

held me

instead.

I learned to plea.

Only to be ignored.

I once thought

you held the world.

I was blind

and didn't se the bomb you held.

A flower cannot

bloom if you

do not nourish it.

With your magnifying

glass you burned

away my self-esteem.

You pulled me

back in with

love songs that

lost their tune.

You shoved affection

down my throat

like it was my

saving grace.

I was drowning

and you let me

suffocate.

We danced to
confusion.
Waltzing through
dead gardens
of flowers.

The words that

were meant for

me,

you freely gave

away to any woman

that caught your attention.

You taught me
to avoid mirrors.
In fear of my
realization of the
woman I could
become.

You plowed into me

with the thought that your

manhood

could fill me with content.

what you didn't know was

that I was left starving.

If my eyes

were the color

of the sea,

would you have wanted

to get lost in

the ocean of

me?

I believed the

mirage like a

wandering fool.

Graciously drinking of

the poison you offered.

As I kneel before you,

unlacing your boots,

massaging the days work

from your feet,

I listen to every word

that falls from your lips.

Every curse of coworkers clings to my heart.

I only wish to make your day better.

I only wish to ease your pain.

I wish to wrap you in the blanket of my love.

Hide from the world until you were ready.

I didn't know that that day would never come.

That that day was only a pipe bomb.

One that would blow our entire existence to high heaven.

We tinkered with the fuse.

Buying time.

Here and there.

Only to forget to enjoy the moments we had.

Love Bomb

Did you notice the

light from my eyes fade?

Or were you blinded by the

beacon of her?

In public you wrap

your arm around my shoulder.

An effort to let everyone

know that I am yours.

My eyes beg

strangers for help.

Warning them that

this display was a ruse.

The idea of unfollowing a woman

whose assets were on display for the world,

correcting the way you speak to female friends,

or the looks that should be reserved for the bedroom

sent you into a frenzy of denial.

Belittling my "insecurities".

Why wouldn't I trust you?

Because you've shown me what always do with it.

– Break it

You searched for Heaven

at the bottom of a bottle.

Taking everything and

leaving but a drop for me.

Whiskey-soaked words

filled my cup.

I pressed it to my lips.

But could never get

drunk enough off you.

Ask the next woman

you meet about

the last time she

feared for her life.

Blankets ripped away,

your voice thunders in malice.

Jolting me awake.

Thorny lips pricked to

keep my eyes wide open.

He took what he wanted from me.

Demanding I obey him.

Degrade me when his needs weren't met.

Dismiss my ambitions and emotions.

I hate the feeling of your gaze running down my naked body. How your hands grab at me. Having used their tenderness on someone else. Bile rises in me. Threatening to expel everything on the floor.

I hate how you demand so much from me. Leaving me hollow inside. How I'm mere property to you. Only here to satisfy your sexual needs.

I hate those songs you play. The beautiful words meant for the one who has captured your heart. That one is not me.

I hate how you lie. Words will set me from. You can't let me leave.

She became silent.

There were no more words to

describe the absence of

emotion within her heart.

She went from being upset,

to arguing,

to feeling nothing at all.

She became silent

because you were

no longer worth fighting for.

The bed held numerous secrets.

It could recall the imprints of bodies.

Relive the hushed moans and whispers.

Echo the cries of anguish.

The bed was a constant reminder of shame, fear, and contempt.

I am Disappointed

The women in your family are known for their strength.

They bring dictators to their knees.

Building empires from the ashes.

They are lioness in the savannah.

Hunting weaker prey.

When their strength is called upon,

they do not roar to the heavens.

They do not congregate.

They do not protect.

They attack with vicious lies.

They give support only to the side of the predator.

Leaving his prey to suffer in silence.

Wishing for death but denied.

Wondering where they went wrong.

Wondering if their actions warranted this fate.

 Pride

You were never
in love with me.
It was the idea
that seduced you.

My symphony was

noise to your ears.

The brilliant colors of
butterfly wings faded
behind the layer of glass.
You wanted to hoard it rarity.
While I longed to fly.

We tried to live by the golden rule.

Treat others the way you want to be treated.

What made you think I wanted to be treated like nothing?

She cried,

"If you had come to me, I would've helped".

There is only so much *talks* can do.

My kindness was your personal fiddle.

Fingers plucked relentlessly,

until every string broke.

The day started as normal. Laughter shrilled through the house. Happiness that couldn't drown out the thundering of my heart. Shay hands made breakfast. Eggs. Sunny-side up. A bacon smile. Reflected what I could not muster. I argued with my thoughts. Pushed down the internal screams that begged me to leave.

I tried to find falsehood in my thinking. Convince myself that I was crazy and nothing was wrong. Bile rose into my throat. Trapping my voice. Squeezing the life of a new beginning out of me. Forcing me to retreat into a shell.

A shell that had been created by you. To keep you comfortable. I struggled to become someone I was never meant to be. I was meant to dance in the rain. Taste its secrets. Someone you made to color in the lines. Never to bleed into the paper. Someone whose light was could not handle.

Quickly, at high-noon, I set out on a new journey. One that had me looking over my shoulder every minute. Worrying that I would see you in the rearview. Coming for me. Ready to drag me back to hell.

A sigh of relief escaped my lips when I saw the mountains. Those beautiful rugged formations welcomed me with open arms. And breathed life into me once again.

"You're safe now".

Words I could not believe.

Concrete walls,

barbed wire,

security cameras.

These are the things

meant to protect me.

Test after test only brought positive results.

The ones that kept us secluded from the outside world.

Covid

Little mouths fed from a serving tray.

Clockwork.

Morning.

Noon.

Night.

Send our regards to the chef.

One day we'll be able to repay them soon.

By the light of the moon,

I let those closest to my heart

know that I am finally safe.

Begged them to never disclose

my location to you.

I recounted the abuse so many times

I can recite it in my sleep.

Nightmares keep me away.

Pushing me to plan my next move.

Like a master chess player,

I move pieces on the board of life.

They came like a thief in the night.

Leaving gifts to make our time more enjoyable.

Tiny hands rip into plastic.

Claiming dolls as their own.

Excited that it felt a little bit like home.

That day called to explain that I did not leave the family that had become my own.

I needed to reassure them that they were still in my heart.

That leaving shattered my soul.

Scattering it across the desert with each mile.

I wanted to hear "I understand" or the declarations on the Pin board were true.

I was not ready to be raked across the coals.

Fire scorched my flesh spat from hate filled tongues.

I couldn't believe that my role model,

who escaped in the dead of night,

demanded I explain why I left.

That my safety meant so little to her.

Tears fell like bullets from a salty Marine.

A proud soldier who I had begged for help claimed,

"Get your mom on your side to help".

Those same lips that insisted his son to change months before.

To put down the bottle and treat his wife with respect.

To quit chasing temporary women and rekindle the fire of love with his wife.

The same people who quickly became my parents were

strangers on the other side of the conversation.

A conversation that once again fell on deaf ears.

I didn't leave you. I left your son.

He never tried to

see things from her perspective.

Never tried to understand why she left.

Broken.

Lost.

Hollow.

He never understood that

he was the root of her suffering.

It must be difficult to

admit that you are

the monster of the story.

I am Struggling

Oh, to be desired!

Not for what is

between my legs but

for the soul what lives inside me.

I shy away from affection

because I have to relearn

to let love in.

To push away every lie

I was taught.

I cower in fear to

show my true colors.

For yours terrified me.

You painted me as

"not all there".

You colored me with lies.

I am told I

took away his

pride and joy.

I took away his control.

I lost track of

how many nights

I cried myself to sleep.

Getting lost in conversations

with the moon.

Asking her if my heart

will ever stop hurting.

"It takes a village",

they say.

What they forget to

mention is that

I am still in

survival mode.

I need a captain to navigate these uncharted waters.

One with a silver tongue.

A man whose mind is as sharp as his saber.

Knowledge his weapon against his deceitful foe.

Hightower

She sought light

as was needed to reveal color,

aslas was bound in

darkness where pigments

remained concealed.

-Toni

I mourn the way things used to be.

Hours of endless laughter.

Getting lost in one another.

How you wouldn't hesitate to dance with me.

I weep for the man that I fell in love with.

The one who cherished me.

My tears soak into the earth,

as I bury these memories.

— Death of a loved one

Blood is thicker than water.

But I was never

your blood and you

never quenched my thirst.

The voice in my

head mimics yours.

It tries to plant doubt

where it is not welcomed.

I wake up gasping.

Memories plague my dreams.

Your hand around my throat.

My most hated piece of jewelry.

Something has awakened within me.

I thought it was gone.

It's terrifying.

"We need to talk".

Four simple words that

make my heart stop in its tracks.

My walls are lined

with stories that you

tried so hard to cover up.

I am Healing

My company is enough

but I know that I am

meant to receive the love I give.

I will never take sunlight for granted again.

After being in the darkness,

I welcome the sun's rays.

It melts away my ice-encased heart.

I never thought I would

be cutting more people

out of my life.

Yet, they keep handing my scissors.

My house is filled with music.

My soul dances freely in the kitchen.

You came into our lives that wonderful year.

A crescent smile and starry eyes.

The voice of a gentle spring day.

Flowers turn towards your sun.

Eager to bask in the warmth of you.

Supportive words watered my child.

Tender hands weed out negativity.

Never allowing it to take root.

Misty

Who knew government was

where I would meet the soul of my soul?

The day you exclaimed,

"We're going to be best friends after highschool!"

left me laughing.

Why would this goddess of

milk and honey want

a peasant like me in her life?

Years passed.

Children expelled from our wombs.

Countless nights of wondering.

How was our counterpart doing?

Dread seized our hearts when silence spanned over months.

Years.

Anger blazed as I was kept from you.

The fear of his rage finally

snuffing out my light kept your awake.

What you didn't know was that I cried for you.

I cried for how I allowed myself to

crumble under his thumb.

I cried because I wasn't strong enough.

"Go. Now."

"Keep going"

"You're safe and that's all that matters".

You were so proud of me.

The hardest part was leaving.

And I did it.

Thank you.

– Sarafina

Loneliness buries itself within my heart.

Slowly, I unearth it.

Reminding myself that I am not lonely for you.

But for the love I never received.

It was a subtle change.

I washed the brown from my hair.

Promising to never be that woman again.

I learned to love myself through your eyes.

You did not see a broken woman.

You saw an angel that still had fight left in her.

A female that grew into her power.

— Sweets

Some people come into

your life to teach you a lesson.

Others come into it to provide solutions.

I thought of you today.

My heart didn't cry in loneliness.

I am content with

my own company.

My time is more

valuable than all

the riches in the world.

You hold on to this dream of reconciliation.

Refusing to see that I have already let go.

I cannot expect to
grow if I do not
nourish myself.

Smile,

Little Miss.

You are one of the best.

You deserve to have a great day.

A wonderful life.

Smile, Little Miss.

As I retold my entire life,

I cried as your heart broke before me.

The kitchen filled with pastries

was thick with anger.

"I should've known.

I would've made she that nothing would've happened to you."

I smile and shake my head.

"I was mean to go through what I did to become the person I am today."

A Master of English.

A scholar of History.

An expert of the mind.

My Guardian Angels on Earth.

The Fates of my life.

Have led me to my final destination.

Wisdom.

Love.

Joy.

These are the lessons I have learned from this trio of women.

Joy.

Love.

Wisdom.

I am enough.

I no longer look over my shoulder in the dead of night.

I no longer fear of the repercussions of my words.

I no longer feel sorry for shining too brightly.

I no longer fear you.

I have learned what it

means to have people

who want me in their presence.

Merely for the safe of being there.

I do not have to prove I am worth their time.

In not have a family to call my own,
one that doesn't see me as expendable,
I have found my tribe.
A group of extraordinary individuals
who have helped in every possible way.
I have found my place in this world.

My daughters will grow
to know that there is a
storm rising within them.
One that will destroy
all barriers set in their way.
My son will grow to know
the importance of being
his sister's ally.
For the cards are stacked
against them from the
day they are born.
My children will grow to
understand that there is
nothing easy about the life
they have been given.
My children will grow to
know that they are the
Masters of their fate.

My inner child can finally rest.

Clean her tear-stained face and

relax into a bed comfort.

We have come a long way, Little One.

I apologize that it too me this

long to get us to Paradise.

I promise that you will

never have to hide away again.

I am Forgiving

I spoke to you for the first time in what felt like years.

I let my words waterfall.

Not letting you to interrupt me.

It was never a question of

"was I enough for you?"

Truth was, I was too much for you.

You could not handle my fire.

You found comfort in simple pleasures.

Unwilling to solve the complexity of me.

The thought of returning to
you leaves me ill.
I will never allow
anyone to control me again.

You have grown into

the man I have waited years for.

I had fought tooth and nail for this result.

When there was no more fight,

I walked away.

Leaving to confront what you had done.

Our years hold a

special place in my heart.

I am grateful for what

has come from them.

Laughter.

Love.

Children.

Family.

Strength.

Triumph.

We balance the scales before us.

Agreeing that our children will

never experience what we did at their age.

I am proud of the person
you are becoming.
The next woman to
enter your life will
rejoice in being yours.

Finally.

After years of miscommunication,

we are able to talk.

Able to listen to one another

without getting into fights off the bat.

Without pointing fingers.

We are finally able to hold ourselves,

as well as each other,

to a standard that we have always wanted.

I brag about the person
you are evolving into to
anyone who will listen.
Why wouldn't I rejoice
in your breakthrough?

You called today to apologize.
I've heard you apologize
before but this was nothing
compared to the past.
Today you didn't need to
be spoon-fed the reasons
of your misbehavior.

We laugh like old friends.

You worry our children will

hate you for what you did to me.

I nod in agreement.

They will be angry.

They will be hurt.

They will be sad.

Then they will be understanding.

They will be grateful.

They will be happy.

2 a.m. calls

because the quiet

becomes too loud.

- Missing the kids

I forgive you.
Without you,
I wouldn't be the person I am.
Without you,
we wouldn't be able to
be the parents we always
wanted to be.

Thank you.